P ETER HUGHES was born in Oxford in 1956. He lived in Italy for several years and continues to find inspiration in Italian literature. He is now based in Cambridge where he runs Oystercatcher Press. He was the 2016/17 Judith E. Wilson Visiting Poetry Fellow at Cambridge University and is a Visiting Fellow at Magdalene College. A *Selected Poems* came out from Shearsman in 2013 and his versions of the complete sonnets of Petrarch were published by Reality Street in 2015. He is currently working on a project inspired by Leopardi whilst continuing to collaborate with poets including John Hall and Simon Marsh.

PETER
HUGHE
S * CAV
ALCANTY
TY * CA
RCANE
TPRES
S

MANCHESTER * MMXVII

First published in Great Britain in 2017 by
CARCANET PRESS LTD
Alliance House, 30 Cross Street
Manchester M2 7AQ
www.carcanet.co.uk

A CIP catalogue record for this book is available
from the British Library: ISBN 9781784103880.

Design: Luke Allan.

The publisher acknowledges financial assistance
from Arts Council England.

Some of these poems have previously appeared in
Litter, *PN Review*, *outLINES* and *Cavalcanty 1–27* (Equipage).
Many thanks to the editors.

'boys only want love if it's torture'
TAYLOR SWIFT

DEDICATED TO *John James*
AND *the memory of Stephen Rodefer*

CAVALCANTY

1

Fresca rosa novella

your shocking pink *tendresse*
electrifies my stick-
iness & spritz of jizzy rhubarb
shoots sap up singing lamb & germ-
ination I now lay/lie at your feet

& your edgy vitality
whose quick strikes
everyone everywhere always
including sheepdogs & bugs
of the field & campsite
reptiles & marsupials
& residents of Devon
have this urge to congregate
at the ends of motorways
to hone extended cover versions
of every track on *Astral Weeks*
in celebration of your alto
tendency to stretch us

you're a super looking human
which is thoroughly inspiring
in that crippling kind of fashion
that first got people visual-
ising angels then etching them
into their own flesh using lumps
of anthracite & millstone grit
tongue tied up delirious fantasies
occupying decades pursuing

the inedible in one
sentenced to plaster over
wounds going right through
one side & out the other

known traditionally as idealism
which has had such a bad press
for decades now protected
by cruisers & airyplanes marked
with the pig-bone logo
but I get idealistic when I see you
redesigning my interiors & out
side spaces & some of that
must be projected into sketches
of the future no matter whose
that then turns out to be
gardens going mental under mis-
translated constellations

2

Avete 'n vo' li fior' e la verdura

how much fruit & veg has been inside you
how many minerals & vitamins
have helped transform the earth & air & light
into your pretty devastating glow
no one should mistake this for the problem
pages of some disingenuous rag
or an outpost of Citizens Advice
straining at the end of someone else's
tether distorting the tissues & bones
the same few words turn liking into love
to quote Shakespeare or maybe Ronnie Scott
on improv or the verve of life in art
we all want to change the great concerti
& play our novel versions on kazoo

3

Biltà di donna e di saccente core

this autumn I Guido Cavalcanti
legendary co-founder of the Dolce
& Gabbana mode of filling colour
supplements & academic footnotes

turn my back on all the peer reviewing
& brash pressures of modern decorum
to look out at the start of a new day
ground damp with dew & sky light with silence

my Southern girl has modified the time
& air available for brainstorming
the strategies & spaces which remain

a possibility between heaven
as it is on earth over the coming
hours & daze of hard-won conjugations

4

Chi è questa che vèn, che'ogn'om la mira

so who's this traversing the piazza
& making waves in the responsive air
& hearts of all in the vicinity
hover on a surge of fresh potential

when her eyes sweep over the actual
inhabitants & trappings of the town
the rest of the attractions vanish back
into the tourist information booth

no one could describe to you how beauty
finds its finest incarnation in her
being out of touch around the corner

we've never been quite bright enough to take
the subtle hints & reassurances
the goddess always hovers round the bend

5

Li mie' foll'occhi, che prima guardaro

Benylin mucus & sardines off toast
nerves in the words read aloud from the start
of the so-called ideas arising
not just as these dots in front of the eyes

but also from the troughs & vibrations
of the line's ear nose & throat department
well also chests & abdominations
& those ripples coming back off the sides

creating such interference patterns
mistaken for the music of your spheres
as fuck she glanced at me over the rim

of whatever I hadn't been thinking
stuck amongst this glaciated landfill
roads from here still closed for reparations

6

Deh, spiriti miei, quando mi vedete

Dante said one nation under a groove
here in Gnawfk Miffy plays with numbers
o clifftop Vodafone reception fail
o bestiaries & lapidaries
for almost every kind of absence
these sunlights mince about upon the sea
their well-known tinsel scintillations wink
back at Debussy etc but
the filthy currents carried you away
so now I know your number off by heart
you ask me not to call or write to say
I didn't know that we would touch that much
I've decided not to accept Martin's
invitation to supper in the hut

7

L'anima mia vilment' è sbigotita

my soul has pressed its nose against this screen
in search of likes & messages from you
or updates on this agonising weight
of time before I get to see your mouth
as well as all its picturesque surroundings
in action in my neighbourhood again
transforming my particularities
into little troupes of dancing iron filings
waving at your stars & their procession
people queueing up to pay for bread turn
& hurt their necks as yours goes sailing by
heavens below I'm bristling with static
& sticking to burned imaginings of
you/me fuse this incandescent circuit

8

Tu m'hai sì piena di dolor la mente

the worst thing about being a dalek
is how remote you feel from tender flesh
& how every sexual position
makes you feel more like a fucking bollard

it's all so weird & inconceivable
that the person strolling past the butcher's
with a bag clogged with Asda ready meals
is set for a night of supple passion

while you stand wheel-clamped by your tinny self
& she's out dancing through the neighbourhood
taking Zumba styling through the city

that never sleeps & never really wakes
I followed the stars & one-way systems
all the way to Ebbsfleet International

9

Io non pensava che lo cor giammai

I didn't think my heart would last the night
you sent me messages I didn't get
the implications of your doubts about
the two of us & several other words
pretty much removed the future perfect
tense & bulging o my decompression
chambers what went wrong with all your washers
& that big round metal handle looked so
secure & resistant to tampering
on the long haul through those senseless decades
before she swam around the edges of my reef
& different parts of me abandoned ship
to drift in shadowed underwater glades
& waver with the rays & weeds & eels

you can't sum up a person using words
neither this woman nor anyone else
is caressed or expressed by any verb
or conjugation & all the music
in Africa fails to convey the pain
of the joy of her love as it inches
past millimetres away from the end
of all your eyelashes & fingertips
this lack of confirmation in her eyes
is what I now clutch to my abdomen
with its packed dreams & kidneys & need for
someone to reconnect my love to skin
I'm waiting for the fucking resurrection
of something that I've never even known

I want to talk about her to the world
of composites & friends from long ago
who mostly died will never hear this song
requested on my breakfast show by no one
yet filling all the air between my ears
a sphere of respite with shimmering walls
the ball an underwater insect clings to
last another night in all this weather
I'm not sure evolution did much good
to balance us here on the very edge
of worlds we've wrecked & what about her mouth
to mouth the passing on of elements
from magical & realistic stories
about great alchemical illusions

song I made you out of early albums
by artists I struggle to remember
I've always been useless at measuring
& estimation & even guessing
but I really need you now to find her
see if she can somehow reassemble
those parts of me that shattered on impact
& ended up dispersed around the town
explain to her how my constituents
are currently littering the district
without her unifying gravity
made up of tenderness & strength & grace
go song & plead with her to come around
& sweep away this fatal installation

10

Vedete ch'i' son un che vo piangendo

I polish off the last of her peach squash
& acknowledge the sounds of some of her
names deep in my throat or whatever it's
called towards these short accommodations

from one periphery to another
shoulder to shoulder with drivers of trucks
& distant relations on the school run
forging indispensable connections
I hold my breath in anticipation
of that little movement of her tongue I
hold her breath & rearrange it in this
awkward new attempt at integration

there used to be a set of plans & risk
assessment procedures with insurance
policies but I've abandoned certain
prototypes & modes of thought forever
following this latest transformation
of the city & her responsiveness
to what the fuck is happening she comes
with new supplies of juice & shuts my mouth

11

Poi che di doglia cor conven ch'i'porti

she reposed behind me with such posture
accomplished cellist that she was she drew
a sword across & deep into my throat
my heavy head relaxed onto her lap
& welcome to the world of Baroque art
Mr Cavalcanty welcome to the
cabaret of bodily effusions
& horrified stares towards the next stage
where I knock up this nativity set
in which the neighbours & local fauna
are encouraged to pause & meditate
upon my vaguely impotent feelings
while we ignore my threads in your velcro
your finer hairs still stuck between my teeth

12

Perché non fuoro a me gli occhi dispenti

sending coded postcards to my lady
of awkward compartmentalisations
now that her pole-dancing days are over
& her interest in art has begun
here's one of me & S. Sebastian
& here's one of my cock in the *bocca
della verità* & this is the end
of yet another phase of hopelessness
not that it hasn't had its miracles
its commas of starlight in the wine glass
the morning moving down her naked back
her fists full of my ordinary hair
I devote the rest of my life to these
bucatini all'amatriciana

13

Voi che per li occhi mi passaste 'l core

contains additional material
for reading groups & cartons of ashes
just go diminutive autoscopy
fast rewind to the start of the tunnel

beyond departments of psychophysics
& the carbonised traces of tinder
she drove through my hedge & into the lounge
creating this derelict extension

interspersed with irregular sections
rafters & yells trashed plasterboard & stars
runes slashed in human hide & toxic air

made inexplicably invisible
to most members of the neighbourhood watch
she shone among the ex-pats of Rapallo

14

Se m'ha del tutto obliato Merzede

I tried community singing
songs about bleached holes
improbable resilience
an empty auditorium
in darkness it's easy to believe
a lyric can have wings
& flutter at the window
dusting to get out
to bring the outside in
for staff training purposes
or help for the swallow
dive through phosphorescence

15

Se Mercé fosse amica a' miei disiri

being manifestations of the whole
history of the planet we each possess
all these walnut-sized knobs of dark matter
swarming with evolutionary forces

exerting pressure just behind the lunch
or late-night snack which fuels the latest
life-defining lunges for those spaces
we imagine past the endings of these lines

or panes or assortments of flimsy walls
& catchments & administrative blocs
plus slag heaps of industrial diseases

burning dreams & generations for a
thimbleful of fat to take onboard
a lifeboat inexorably sinking

16

A me stesso di me pietate vène

& still my cogs emit this high-pitched whine
although they never mesh with the planet's
transmission systems or anyone else
portrait of the artist as a duff clutch

so I'm stuck between vibrating mayhem
& a car that's never heading down the road
Christ it's like I've got Elmore James playing
right in the tips of each of my fingers

with none of the sound ever getting out
through the skin or sudsy Marigold gloves
sink kitchen isolated house or town

it's already the end of whatever
they're calling this period nowadays
& what you hear here is just an echo

17

S'io prego questa donna che Pietate

I think therefore I am feeling thoughtful
& yet too inattentive to complete
this nasty cross-stitch picture of the queen
or paint my charity-shop figurine

of possibly a bear or hedgehog sat
on its cold hindquarters drinking nothing
from a wide bowl it might be a racoon
well talk about cold fucking pastoral

that old autumn feast of Dionysus
got really out of hand again last year
& still they're finding celebrants in trees

ponds & the skip in which I'm dreaming of
Tiepolo in the Labia palace
o how I miss eating you between meals

18

Noi sian le triste penne isbigotite

just as a hoovered keyboard will bristle
for days with static & indignation
or a pencil will never be sharpened
when the lead's smashed down to the chewed red end

& pens with blue or green ink always leak
on parts of the hand that haven't touched them
& we have to give up wondering why
italic nibs are best for sculpting cheese

& all the metaphoric language smacks
of disconnected desperation &
random items from the inventory

hold hands & hover in a translucent
soft blob of ineffective superglue
well this is how I'm feeling when you've gone

19

I' prego voi che di dolor parlate

I know you've all had a lot on your minds
but I thought you might like to take a break
from your issues to concentrate on mine

which include dry rot & whistling gaskets
& an ache in the gut that's calling out
for Dyno-Rod I am these sensations
of someone else's knuckles just behind
my eyeballs which is making it tricky
to gaze reflectively upon the world
or freshen up the stale pits of my mind

& that's a shame because I'd seen some sights
& enjoyed a stunning range of inputs
which had made my mind feel like a fountain
playing incessantly throughout the nights
of a small piazza in the ghetto
instead of one of those tiny red lights
on the extension lead under the desk

I've reached that stage when glimpses of justice
& gorgeousness such as fresh leaf on beech
or any member of the cod family
proper policy her face & music
sending these little ripples through the wine
hurt my eyes & render me rickety
knowing their value & fragility

20

O tu, che porti nelli occhi sovente

it is 3:25 in Hunstanton
& a book I threw out of the window
stays rigorously frozen to a leek
I threw from nowhere like these 'sentences'
ice music spells ice music spells ice muse
why does a radio suddenly stop
tuning into anything but adverts
Tory transfer deals & drifts of white noise
we interrupt this broadcast to bring you
havoc in the hearts of all our punters
wonder why the paperwork is shredded
& carted away by rodents & draughts
to a dark nest of chilly litter where
Francesco di Gregori sings goodnight

21

O donna mia , non vedestù colui

another Cornish pasty clogged with swede
completes its earthly journey to the drains
punch-drunk with germs & sales pitch we emerge
from one of Satan's anuses (Ryan
Air FR4952) & into
the cooling cave of the Perugino
bar & grill where an old television
is murmuring suave updates on Gaza
trade in *Being & Nothingness* for an
Amazon gift card of up to eighty-
one pence & try to keep despair at bay
for as long as it takes to finish this
tinny beer & unpredictable night
& whatever is left of tomorrow

22

Veder poteste, quando v'inscontrai

a disadvantaged potato plant grows
from a sliver of peel in the black bin
where it will live out its nights & then die
in a minimal fuss about nothing
I dreamt she sat for Alan Macdonald
in a flicker of chiaroscuro
an ill-lit lyric cut by its own knife
in the spirit of one hapless punter
so that is what those songs were all about
& this the home of metaphors of loss
& here the acid lash of memory
February rain on a plastic lid
a phone ringing in a distant city
I know it might as well have fed the pigs

23

Io vidi li occhi dove Amor si mise

thus love scared the fuck out of everyone
with a pristine & glistening layer
transforming the page into a skid pan
& merging all the byways & borders

the gritters are out – a voice haunts the skies
weep blood or some exotic oxide &
perhaps we walked a little way together
past the flattened boxes of the city

I still see her stop under the street light
& turn to look at me as if blessing
some unrecognisable passer-by

possibly the victim of a mugging
or maybe someone who'd missed the last flight
& had no other way of getting home

24

Un amaroso sguardo spiritale

I'm buoyed by her enthusiastic glance
in my direction that was actually
aimed at something random far behind me
so I'm surging towards nothing once again
tail wagging lips whistling throwing caution
& perspective to the customary
winds of change which flick grit & hopelessness
into my own impercipient eyes
while carrying any local music
away from the zones of habitation
far out over these seductive marshes
where the lights of doggers & illusions
mingle with the mist & strange reflections
will guide me down the tracks to closing time

Posso degli occhi miei novella dire

well lookee here – it's the shock of the new
much like the schlock of the old recycled
into fresh articulations of desire

so where the fuck does all this leave us now
with our colour-coded interdental
prongs & maladjusted memory cards
& HSBC voiceover artists
sticking fists up wooden politicians
to take the lead in steering modern art
learning health & the prospects of our love

proffer spectacular encouragement
to gargle & rock with whiskey & fire
gnaw on each of the safety rails & chew
through every stanchion of the landing stage
I like a salad as much as the next
panda but this time I'm engulfing trees
rafters & the roof of my own mouth

press send to flick this language through the sky
in the hope it sticks to some equipment
to which she may remember the password
& log-in details – she could read it once
then delete it forever the same way
she cancelled our multicoloured futures
& left me with this draft in black & white

26

Veggio negli occhi de la donna mia

I understand the situation babe
I hang around here to help this poem
keep its head above the churning waters
still feeling all the reverberations

from the first time I entered us & slid
my fingers through your wings & shuddering
find it hard to keep my concentration
when all the little details don't add up
to even the sum of their parts I can't
envisage an enduring logo or
leading intellectual abstraction poised
above the crumbling gates of our theme park

I love to see you walking through the world
between fast-food outlets & substantives
nearly dislocated from our hunger
for life & upgraded definitions
of what it will have been to vivify
the only mornings afternoons & nights
provided to the living for some months
spent staring through a range of open doors

27

Donna me prega – per ch'eo voglio dire

now the lady makes me think about love's
pit-bull attacks on the soul's soft tissues
& those fatal core-reactor meltdowns
& deep immunity to metaphor
it's tricky thinking through these things in ink
as love demands we loosen up our grip
on pre-existing modes of consciousness
affiliation & self-confidence
otherwise we stand no chance of melting
flowing into fresh configurations
in response to love's accommodations
of feral power rerouted through refined
reformulations of specific lips
in actual laps tomorrow evening

so what about the inner baklava
comprising thousands of translucent veils
crushed nuts honey dust experiences
weird terms softly brushed with olive oil &
clarified I can't believe I haven't
come yet her hair against the troubled light
trembling phone crawls right across the table
towards the rest of the rest of the world
love becomes a bustling mental impulse
with overactive elbows forever
nudging past *tutti* & barging its way
to the front of any queue or crowd
to snatch the finest view
of what's about to happen which is nothing

short of mysterious how love is made
of nothing yet feels like marble knuckles
kneading your most vulnerable hollows
articles & raw protuberances
into a species of blue Slush Puppie
or one of the ghostly breakdown trucks of
the apocalypse towing you at speed
the wrong way through a maze of one-way streets
by night so you can barely stay on-board
that dilapidated unicycle
it's not how they portrayed it in the films
with all those unpolluted beaches or
luminous farm-free meadows without snakes
or hip umber bookshops in Manhattan

love enjoys an absence of perspective
well enjoys in the sense of despairs at
a heady blend of claustrophobia
seasickness & agoraphobia
are the least disagreeable symptoms
alongside earache in the genitals
dizziness & backache down the front
you keep receiving mental messages
from poets & energy companies
emergency services & phantoms
trees & insects send you final demands
the stars ask for your help with a survey
the pope calls to say if you eat those eels
you are bound to die – sorry wrong number

so love carves out an empty space which aches
to be refilled by interference waves
to vast notions in everyday persons
do what they can to keep this thing alive

through radio dedications & good
will a little card or bloom & bottle
of prosecco or on this occasion
a thoughtful Rosso di Montefalco
has moistened the tablecloth between us
& dripped on these scribbles in the notebook
lending a welcome chromaticism
to the usual black-&-white deceptions
which established almost every action
in our lives throughout the run-up to today

off you go young poem without dragging
a heavy tail of clever dickery
just leave without the usual excuses
drive on along anonymous ring-roads
let's stop now while the bar is still open

28

Pegli occhi fere un spirito sottile

I'd say as a general rule it's better
to steer clear of general rules & think
about specific situations which
are usually metamorphoses
such as the translation of Mario
Balatelli from Italian to
Liverpool or the drone over Paris
on July 14th being filmed as
it filmed & occupying many fucked-
up genres encouraging us to stuff
our fists deeper in each other's pockets
or how you march your troops right through my ghosts
know there are things you can do with a horn
that nobody has done with just a spoon

Una giovane donna di Tolosa

of all the various accounts of how
my pilgrimage was interrupted I
recommend the third or maybe the fourth
which emphasises where the rhythm comes
from unexpected sex & the deceased
plus a little early Dr Feelgood
she could have the church of fucking England
rocking in the aisles & cloisters etching
contemporary updates of Paul Klee's
Little World (1914) or any-
body's little world this evening my blood
comes coursing back around the bend to see
if the head has any news for the heart
or other departments & yesterday
I heard her voice is echoing inside

30

Era in penser d'amor quand'i'trovai

we met these girls on holiday
the visually-impaired one sang
it's raining
men

it's good to have a break
from the diurnal
a drink or two
I told them of my Southern girl
& pointed out
the bell won't ring
it's upside down
& now holds all my water

they shared rum
looks as I outlined
my land-cress project
& I explained
she manages to pack more anchovies into a cello
than anyone else in Cadiz

they claimed the stars were whispering in dialect
& that the last translator passed away a hundred years ago
just after his children
worked their passage to New York
then crossed the moonlit plains
to some forgotten centre
that used to have a different name

the track wound on through woods
& vinyls to Bishop's Stortford
crossing weeks of heathland
tenanted with gorse & pallid birch
before swaying on slippery slopes
throughout the first of these ultimate days
where we dip a brush in honey
& hold it up against the light

& then the nights grew longer
you couldn't move for bats & spinach
it's been so long since I smoked one of these
& any words remaining
have all turned into moths
we do need feet
we don't need all these shoes

so southwards ho   young songlet
see if you can wend your way
towards the lap of the imagined
see if you can nestle in her precincts
& voice the general predicament
encourage her to ease her agile limbs
& spirits into warmer inclinations
& some soft moist acknowledgement

31

Gli occhi di quella gentil foresetta

I locked on to her signals which then stopped
& which I probably imagined in
the first & second places where we met

every time I see her knocks more bright cliffs
off of the wet end of my glacier
& having no access to replacements
my being diminishes & dribbles
like some run-over ice pop in the sun
outside her garage if you look closer
it's easy to trace the tracks of her tyres

if there's a smile on my face it's because
of the music clearly & a gladness
she exists though unavailable to
me gladness a bright buoy in a grey sea
ice water whispering interiors
threatening to overcome settlement
agriculture & civilisation

I especially remember the speed
& dexterity of her thumbs as well
as several things I used to do with mine
as she flew over into the darkness
of our deactivated purposes
& the shacks of her own expectations
& the desolation of this sentence

my gladness she exists a high harmonic
on the complex chord of what is this thing
although it doesn't matter what it's called
now the low-lying meadows are flooded
where we once walked through unexpectedness
on a morning she may not remember
all the places where nothing now may grow

32

Quando di morte mi conven trar vita

what to do about these nuns with road rage
& why should I suffer
more than anyone else
just because I'm the first person singular

perched upon this resonating reed   or
eerily vibrating gangplank canti-
levered out across the cold polluted
depths & swells of death
it is hard to be wholehearted
in my nth appearance as a third-rate one-man band
or maybe fourth basically the plan now
is for the band to split up & head off
in various directions due to those
artistic differences & ego issues

she stands there in the gloaming with her spam
dragon & all my anachronisms
poorly disguised as dusky shrubbery
nor can I remember if it was me
or Fred Buscaglione who first sang
criminalmente bella to her mouth
& launch-pads well the dangers of flying
too close to her super-heated sources
are well documented but now I freeze
& where the snows of autumn are is here

rearranging the universe is tough
& probably best left until morning

when the power of this Bricco has worn off
obviously the heart burnishes itself
& that which it loves when it loves like this
destructively so as to have a gap
for miles around in which a song may sound
& get some echoes moving off in her
direction fraught with rumpus & whispers
tomorrow needed her to mouth each word

33

Io temo che la mia disaventura

I'm afraid that all my disadventures
in wonderland have brought me to despair
& reality with its numb markets
featuring knocked-off hoover-bags & rust
certain thoughts get so entangled in the brain
that they can never be extirpated
except by utterly changing one's pub
service providers & default settings
phone contract & energy companies
preferred kinds of wine whiskey & dark rum
banks supermarkets cheese-browsing habits
facial & pubic coiffeur maybe from
landing strip to helicopter pad but
the carousel will not stop going round

La forte e nova mia disaventura

I have to admit that this most recent
catalogue of fuck-ups has impacted
on even my deep-seated sense of love

we've already established that my life
has been effectively dismantled by
her tendency to listen to her head
while I'm like let's dive off this shop &
have an oceanic evening dip
though there's no water for miles & the kids
have made themselves a bonfire in the bedroom

Doug Oliver McSweeney Crozier
Chaloner Harwood followed John Riley
& what about all of these great ageing
poets who've yet to let us in on all
the answers so I Google Roy Fisher
& JHP then email several friends
to check that they've survived another night

most of them seem to think they're still alive
though P. Riley says he'll check with Beryl
John James winks back over the BBQ
the lights are going out all over my
phone then coming back on again I fill
a glass with a modest portion of Ciù
Ciù Bacchus & hum along to night sleet

go words through extractor fans & cat flaps
go & ride unseasonable spring weather
go & ride the fumes & random slipstream
kicking backwards off each departing car
go in no particular direction
her blinds are drawn her television on
she wouldn't hear you even if you called

35

Perch'i' no spero di tornar giammai

I don't think I'll ever be returning
but then I'm not a poem
there's nothing to stop you going
as an attachment or by snail mail
or a page in yet another pamphlet
she may bookmark with a faint smear of ash

you could tell her how my writing hasn't
really evolved much in the last few months
& how I'm still banging on about her
idealised shit in ways which would get
on even Robert Graves' various tits
her wonderful this & marvellous that
even though her this & that were stunning
it's a good idea to keep up the tone
trying to be blithe instead of bitter
act responsibly with all these letters

in spite of all the paracetamol
& locally produced expectorant
I can still hear my own heart in my ear
knocking down the gates like an army of
barbarians or Tory candidates
who look to reinstate the medieval
wastes they mistake for civilisation
they turn my poems into confetti
for the thriving county-wedding business
where everyone still comes in fancy dress

so I'll be Mills & you be Boon & grant
me one more opportunity to grind
our separated seconds into prime
flour ready for the fucking kitchen
of dreams dissolving into these grey days
& what the fuck should I dress up as now
a zen market-gardener on acid
a member of the regional undead
keeping to the shadows after sunrise
becoming reacquainted with silence

in another part of the universe
a dozen seed potatoes are chitting
on a windowsill where my elbow rests
I'd like to remain a custodian
of hope but the earth keeps growing new stones
& every day returns to darkness
go song with the ghosts of Saturday night
go at the helm of a crippled trolley
go with the ashes of my sanity
go song with this grasshopper in a tin

36

To Dante: Certe mie rime a te mandar vogliendo

Hi Dantz – hope you're not partying too hard
I was going to send you these poems
about my heart going through a juicer
when love looking like death smashed down the door
shouting: 'stop – don't be such an idiot!'
I need a little feedback from someone
I exclaimed *so why shouldn't I email*
Dante though his blog is getting heavy
'he just can't cope with unrequited love –
some of those lines of loss will break his heart'
whispered the cadaverous countenance
'the only audience for your whingeing
is me & the one who's deaf to your words
& some who you may haunt when you are gone'

37a

Dante Alighieri to love's faithful followers:
A ciascun' alma presa e gentil core

& a shout-out to all you lovesick souls
with battered hearts who never get their head
around the fact that to abseil without
a rope will nearly always end in tears
it's late enough to be the early hours
whether you're in love or Newport Pagnell
I regained consciousness parched & haunted
by a monster who said its name was Love
at first it seemed full of the joys of spring
as it clutched my heart in one of its claws
while my Madonna slept slumped in its arms
but then Love made her wake up with a start
& fed her with torn-off chunks of my heart
before it rinsed its bloody hands & left

37b

Guido's response: Vedeste, al mio parere, onne valore

you should lay off the cheese before sleeping
especially those blue-veined savages
which rustle when you hold them to your ear
then sing a little song about decay
& elopement by elephant at night
below the endless stellar procession
I find that when I'm rocking on my porch
singing something simple to the banjo
which keeps reminding me of Sappho &
a one-legged duck swerving past the trout
& those guest beers that outstayed their welcome
it's easy to forget the source & spring
you know who I mean – she looks a lot like
that one who wasn't in the sugarbabes

38a

wouldn't it be great if a few poets
including you & me obviously
could hang out in a hot-air balloon &
live with our heads in the clouds along with
some other organs & maybe hampers
& rain-capture units & ideally
wi-fi as well as a stash of something
soothing to sip inhale or listen to
not just poets either I mean we'd need
our indispensable partners in crime
or possibly her from number thirty
& we could while away the hours with talk
of love & high-class versification
hey Guido you're not even listening

38b

S'io fosse quelli che d'Amor fu degno

if I were lucky enough to be loved
by love which I can't even remember
then a shared cruise on your well-stocked balloon
would now be far too tempting to refuse
but just because you're always buoyed by hope
for some unearthly apotheosis
or high excursion off with the fairies
can never mean that I could float off too
my heart is just too heavy to ascend
in some flimsy wickerwork contraption
borne aloft by nothing more than hot air
I'm also susceptible to Cupid
& an easy target for his arrows
that's the last thing you need when ballooning

39

Se vedi Amore, assai ti prego, Dante

o for a centigram of pethidine
spiralling through a shot of stemetil
to keep the feeling of the world beyond
beyond these impenetrable forests

of nerves & upended expectations
some of the originals are mummified
recycled burned deleted or shredded
up & down the dead neck of history

it's no good looking here for rumours of
correspondences / authenticity
dead sea scrolls / leaflets advertising pizza

the music of listening to the music
is one more set of roadworks in your head
obstructing your return to where you are

40

Dante, un sospiro messagger del core

time is always running in & pointing
its spectacularly crusty baguette
towards the shops where you forgot the mushrooms
& where one evening you will lose your head
once more along with your wallet & sense
of direction & identity though
what I want to know now is vanishing
to be replaced by restless ghosts & thirst
on this side of the anonymous night
I'm treading choppy waters in my sleep-
lessness which leaves me dampened & exhausted
an easy victim for the octopus
of love which occupies its lair & mine
cracking open every heart & mollusc

41

I'vegno 'l giorno a te 'nfinite volte

I think of you a thousand times a day
& every time I do I go downhill
at unexpected angles as they call
the latest British entries in the slalom
ice melts around the entrance to my lair
while thugs with clubs assemble on the lawns
to savour sherry & resume the hunt
for even weaker members of the species
the heavens do mango & passionfruit
with no added sugar a culvert fills
& damp spring comes roaring through the hedgerows
but I've opted to stay in the shadows
of my own taverna & reflections
with an old tin full of stars & echoes

42

Certo non è de lo 'ntelletto acolto

back then I still knew how to keep my tongue
out of the way of my teeth but these days
everything gets stuffed into the mincer
& ground into a fabricated paste
repackaged as a version of the past
deforestation of my gnawed uplands
still attracts stimulating subsidies
as long as my scuffed & wizened heart stays
stuck in the recovery position
for the best & worst chunks of a lifetime
spent exploring these unforgiving plains
where we chew the acrid cud of language
for a year or two more then drift away
light feathers on the breath of God's old dog

43

Gianni, quel Guido salute

breathe in & feel the latest crop of stones
migrating through the soil towards the light
consignments of attenuated skies
no-fly zones & compromised compartments
observe the dissolution of the heavens
& their gradual withdrawal from this
cavalcade of national degradation
their mouths stuffed full of other people's plums
with regard to your recent enquiry
I can confirm that I am still writing
& my motivation remains the same
I restring the bow that you'll remember
soon John James & the courgettes will return
to drink deeply once more to the nameless

44

Ciascuna fresca e dolce fontanella

when the goddess of anachronism
hovers on the margins of my vision
resplendent in a mesmerising blend
of woad-tinged accessories & kevlar
look she advises – gesturing vaguely
in the direction of my compost heap –
I bring you exemplary suggestions
buck the fuck up & cease your hankering
it is time to manoeuvre your mojo
through this opening into the real worlds
to be revitalised by that which is
instead of being bled by long distance
expeditions after the imagined
the recycled & the illusory

45

Se non ti caggia la tua santalena

one thing about this speed awareness course
(bring your own lunch) is that I find myself
back in late Janáček who rows against
the current which carries her away thus
creating some illogical whirlpools
which also drift away towards the past
& those night closures south of Kettering
& further complications with the cat
& what will become of all this music
I wonder what happened to her cello
I keep tripping up on a level path
& banging my head against these echoes
where souvenirs of myth & namelessness
glisten in the inner ear for ever

In un boschetto trova' pasturella

let's tip the fridge into this tupperware
& translocate into the camper van

whose little swinging forest-glade dalek
air freshener & fine dope-head paint job
featuring Gong plus brass-section Clangers
urge us on to sample new sensations
& rearrange the mistranslated stars
before their final privatisation

these days it's best to take your own cosplay
shepherdess & lunch to avoid tricky
misunderstandings & mine are tangled
up with more street furniture than she can
shake a crook at the tongue-tied predictions
of Nosferatu never do come true

so where is all this going going gone
proceeding to the movement of the blown
& occupied white poplar whispering
some indistinct responses in the mid-
June winds of change in which it orchestrates
the voices of the sky by night & day

when perky finches don't have time to stop
& listen to the press releases while
I stretch in some sun-flooded piazza
& see her slowly turning in a room
frescoed by Pinturicchio & still
smiles in awe & wondering forever

47

Da più a uno face un sollegismo

cars approach from opposite directions
then pass & slowly disappear from view
described afresh in passages of Bach
as are my procedures in the kitchen
it's a new day in an ageing decade
the ear canal feels full of rusty bikes
there are no maps for this territory
the best way to proceed is by making
a continuous web of connections
to local protuberances & then
rhythmically swinging in the direction
of the music or Spiderman echoes
& tantalising scents of home cooking
until you fly right through the end of the line

48

Una figura della Donna mia

I am ready to purchase a singlet
beyond the goldfish bowl of the cosmos
the fictitious gods are awarding points
to all the daft protagonists below
they watch soot settle on peanut butter
in a kitchen that's now devoid of life
they read several more pages of Dante
& wish the universe were that clear-cut
dude in the subway was singing our song
remembering how we fucked each other
up babe is practically a full-time job
& the sensation of washing your hair
for the first time after a fierce haircut
is what it feels like seeing you again

La bella donna dove Amor si mostra

they gave the cat a Viking burial
hacking out a cat flap in the cello
then inserting their rigid companion
sleek in its marinade of lighter fuel
& setting the redundant instrument
– all those hours of practice come to nothing –
alight & adrift on a turning tide
to the strain of Elgar on an iPod
meanwhile back in my backyard I break up
my burned texts of Petrarch & *The Ashes
of Gramsci* insensitively blended
with some early Guido Cavalcanti
all firmly tamped into the pepper mill
then ground onto this dish of bucatini

50

Di vil matera mi conven parlare

Frank Landini's on the Graham Norton
Show again & *Hello* magazine is
fluffing up more features on Dante's loft
& begging him to take part in *Strictly*
much of the world or my head has gone off
another monophonic ballata
is whingeing its way across the airways
the city is diminishing each day
stub it out before it burns your fingers
it's time to refurbish the motorhome
& have a quiet word with the neighbours
how to think the thought of transformation
begins to energise this phase of night
before the sun comes up & chars these pages

51

Guata, Manetto, quella scrignutuzza

time is running in from the surrounding
newsagents & galaxies continue
to give themselves a bit of space to source
our hybrid replenishment of presence
contains too many plosives doesn't it
beauty finds its finest incarnations
in laid-back collaborations where one
note comes in swift response to one of yours
& vice versa although the music splits
in all senses of the words reproduce
& echo sounds no one has ever heard
hence the compelling force of the quartet
which began as a fraught sketch but became
a record of a world which now has ended

52

Novelle ti so dire, odi, Nerone

the ethereal beauty of slender
rhubarb skin curls in a green bowl of cold
water is so rarely celebrated
therefore more wonderful this afternoon
the tart aroma of leopard urine
will never disappear from your garden
& these vaults of attenuated chants
have stopped me from listening to reggae
I am so looking forward to Shakespeare
not to mention Proust & Pasolini
happy are they who discover today
they're younger than Isabelle Adjani
ciao irradiated polarities
it is time to deconsecrate the verb